FROM NATURE

# FROM NATURE

## ALAN BERNHEIMER

CUNEIFORM PRESS

2019

Cover photograph by Alan Bernheimer

Some of these poems first appeared in *The Spoonlight Institute* (Adventures in Poetry, 2009); *Across the Margin*; *Annex Press*; *Big Bell*; *clash of the lichens*; *Dreamboat*; *For Bill, Anything*; *Hambone*; *mark(s)*; *Periodic Postcard*; *Sal Mimeo*; *Shiny*; *The Delineator*; *The Equalizer*; *The Sienese Shredder*; *TRY*; and *Way Bay*. Many thanks to the editors.

Cuneiform Press titles are distributed to the trade by
Small Press Distribution in Berkeley, California
spdbooks.org

ISBN: 978-0-9860040-8-7
cuneiformpress.com

I. SLEEPING WITH SIRENS

I

SLEEPING WITH SIRENS

BREAKFAST

Forgetting words
The moment you
Hear or read them

Is one way to avoid
Plagiarizing but just
Keep their flavor

And then try
Expressing that
In your own words

As if you could
Own words
You can't even

Keep thoughts
From slipping away
They're the slipperiest

Of all the slippery
Things in life
The hotel elevator

That rises way
Past the roof
And slips across

A higher landscape
A different neighborhood
Why not ask

If any of these
Places will be
Open for breakfast

# THE TRUTH ABOUT MORE

Everyone is an intellectual
Whose words can be exchanged for cash
Mothballs dissolved in vodka

Anesthetize the agent
Only the mercury is true
How can I believe in that

Social world of tone
Metal & celluloid novelties
Philosophy should come out to play

A guy with imagination gets pictures in his head
Like there's no tomorrow
A word that means itself

The red patches on black are visible
As the whales tango through the lagoon

MANY STARS AND ONE'S PERPETUALLY SHOOTING
*for Alli Warren*

Eyes have it for the dream sequins
At weepy random lengths gone to
Wasted years so close behind

Now what about rhyme detection
Completes yourself by proxy
Identity parade in footloose stride

And already beans coming out of my ears
Don't show stored form warning
I've got all day with least astonishment

It's nothing to turn round
And go back two or three
Miles to cross your Ts

Everybody looks at the sky
Tell us about your lute

DECAF EMOJI

Have I lost my delighted attitude
With telescoping pencils and recorded atmosphere

The shadows are having fun
Getting a hush on

Apologies for inconvenience
Keeping dignity under hat

Palpably concocted and
Tributary to the wind

It's anyone's guess
Swimming into sight
At the heart sleeve club

While some good will mines patience
From a racing perspective

The scenery looks better
Without you in it

Faint mowing at the edge of sound
Fugitive thoughts

Struggle to divide the air
Celery and violets
Sunday morning emptiness

Whom fortune has not blessed
Still rages and weeps

IPSATUDE

> *for Tim Atkins & Jeff Hilson*

Everyone's secret life
Inside head fake
Get out more

Forget to forget
View from locker
Twenty watt brain

Looks at sky
One of punching nuns
Ants see molecules

Shady side up
I'll be taking names
Shoe on other foot

But badly bent
Read up write down
Haven't heard boo

Crimea river
Use for ransom
Stripped like this

Needle in thigh
Patinated bronze
Fat encircled eyes

Anything you want
Tricked the starter
Me Geppetto

Gorgeous rolling hills
Best dressed man
In for it now

Tiger balm wrench
Some way out
Habit of mind

Live fast
Leave beautiful archive
Everyone's sex life

Touched by movies
Fix torn sprockets
Signs of prowl

Inside business
Pushing electrons
Battery angst

About our adventure
Ulteriority
Falls into faux

Smack dab
Metabolic grief
Taller of the two

Wants to be friends
Don't go there
Invent perspective

Items you want
Lack means for comedy
Set up as new

Distance sensation
Needs more jewels
Muscular lens focus

Rearrange universe
No end to machinery
Knock self out

Stick ups in demand
World of triggers
War of tug

Blind spot for dance
A matter of time
Next performance review

Cellophane cocktail
Walk in the woods
Got all day

Skirting with disaster
Think on feet
Not without mustard

That for pills
Paid by word
Brook no denial

From third base
Sane and shapely
Who don't belong

Contain the truth
Out of anything
That darling blue

Greek infinity
Talk self in
Comes from spine

Ask for Dennis
Philosophical garnish
On the lam

Intrigue each other
Out on limb
Postcard touch

Steps to wipe
Away your image
Came to grief

More than this
Like as not
Lid off life

Croupier manicure
Over and took
Placeholder enclave

Has no way
On the tarmac
Play the sap

Look at works
Test routine
Send you over

HISTORY OF HAPPINESS

Just did the math
Too birds eye for me
Living by wits

Miss out what's said
Travel size heartthrob
Gravity situation

Confess stupid alibis
Unemployed emotions
Keep healthy distance

Showy brushwork
Rakish dogma
Skirmish in the archives

Equanimity overrated
All puffed up
Homer at home

Sorry for what
Clumsy miscues
Put miles in air

Up for the count
Hero worship
Had a way with clouds

Call it a truce
Misery loves misery
Dispatch illusion units

What mood says
Disappearing zeroes
Tiny white flecks

World's worst blank
Animal episode
Next undercurrent

Words mean everything
Put skids under you
Waiting for emptiness

To fill with thought
Thought with words
Would he has been

Racking up karma
Knock the dents out
For extra oomph

Every element
Something to someone
Smoke in the shade

Naughty or Naugahyde
Spasms of youth
Dead for a ducat

Curious gray eyes
Would be my department
Touching another drop

People want to be
Spoken to as a snowflake
Settle down to business

Top dog hot tub party
Got the burg closed up
Author's compliments

Magpie fragment
Be a nuisance
The long meow

# TWILIGHT OF THE TRILOBITES

Where did existential leave its beret
Attracting us like monks to fame

The world is run over by angry
Men with ambiance units

Tremors in the awning
Extending ovals into space

Whatever intervenes is artistry
Someone says you have nice hands

Reality has a transparent center
Inside layers of shiny candor

The beach looks good today
Like spraying ether

But your empty eyes see
So many smoke rings

FUTURAMA
*for Bill Berkson*

The difference between
truth serum and asterism

The dark of the matinee
and fathomably lovely

dirigible shadow moving
at dirigible speed across

the 1920s Oakland Tribune
facade a year ago today

Apartment life with caper delivery
just around the cornice

Maybe Monk in Oslo
and elevator men at this remove

*When we watch the flight of a bird, a part of the flight
seems to be occurring at the present instant, and a part to
have occurred prior to the present instant.*
—E.R. Kelly

What sorts of things are instants of time

Are events metaphysically basic

If we lived forever would there be a sense of time

Is time fossilized in the structure of language

Can time be completely empty

Are events pairs of a sentence that is true

Is the present made out of time

Can folk reject time theory without changing the topic

Is time our escape from contradiction

Can events recur or persist

Why is no sense assigned to time

Must participants exist when writing events occur

Are more assumptions than needed to get the job done
    ontologically extravagant

Is time a manifold of metaphysically basic points

Are we ideologically committed to the present being special
    or specious

IBIS IN EGYPT
*for Robert Harris*

Put paper in the past
Like a fish at night

A huge circling above
The polished Nile

Softer water closer shave
Wiseness in the noise

Everybody's somebody's fool
Apologize for inconvenience

Before I forget flirtatious
Spaces and tales of place

Dirty ice on the side
What's the matter with this line

Prehistoric peeps find middle
Ground and wallow in it

No better place for learning
About stars than stir

It's not all damaged logic and
inspiration at every breath

PROTECTED WITNESS
*for Aaron Simon*

You want to look
Good in green
Your whole life

Crisp and cryptic
Not a person
Who can't spend change

Or act like a pronoun
Any good at smiling
A little oblivion

Goes a long way
With immense solos
Cluttering terrains

But current stuff is lots more fun
Too busy to be human
One more at a time

CELEBRITY ALTERATION

Other people's wisteria
Fails to unlock past
So many lime-lit whitewalls
Even Pinkertons have to sleep
Problem is the material
Keeping self company
Fits a lot of descriptions
Emotional outcast
Concourse of atoms
Hard to have posthumous fun
You people are filled with
Trace amounts of mystique

SHOOT HOOKY
*for Jason Morris*

Man talking to sky
What you gotta do
Aim at the eyes

It is possible
That suspense never ends
Make bed lie in it

No matter laughing
Everything but the molecule
People don't appreciate

The substance of things
I look like someone you've met
More in the past

Wading through kaftans
As though hating it
Who believe in misty ways

Would bet my depot
Or use much backup
Long since lost the plot

THE NEW SENTIENCE

It feels great being anyplace
Replete with exterior décor
Secret springs of action

Head airing out inside scenery
Life's passage was never going to be fearless
And abundance of caution

Behooves not backing leg shows
You didn't have to be square to resist Cubism
Every building claims it was a brothel

We march monarchy carefully
Through the trepidation of society
The past unspools beneath

Lunch for two dinner for six
Alive with pithful words
And thrilling ones of swing

You need any help with the coffin
It's going to be feathery till she comes to

SEALS SLEEPING

Seals sleep as they sink in the sea

Seal sleeping underwater then waking up

How seals sleep with only half their brain

Seals sleeping stock photos

Half-awake seals help explain sleep disorder

How does SEAL Team 6 get to sleep

Seals sleeping between the rock stock footage

Elephant seals sleeping royalty free

Mack's ear seals earplugs

Crabeater seal still sleeping

Apnea ashore and at sea

Madness seals the deal for sleeping with sirens

Sleeper sharks snag sleeping seals

Diving seals and meditating yogis

Sleeping seals and stonechats

Nice marine seals sleeping on the snow in Antarctica

Seals, wall art, and home décor

II

# BEAUTILITIES

## THE SCAFFOLDING PATRIARCH

A signal for help draws a private pilot from her course. Weaving the plane through some tight city streets, I turn into one that is an impossible web of ironwork several stories high. To avoid a crash I latch onto a piece and find myself standing up in some elaborate scaffolding that is just now being dismantled. All sign of the victim seems to have disappeared. The scaffolding comes down with the amazing speed of roustabouts pulling down a big top and I see, now from the ground, that the efforts are directed by a young patriarch, whose orders are keenly followed by the family squad. The key is a quickly locked or unlocked joining device that he adapted from the daffodil game of football. Everyone is astounded when he announces a street party to follow the completion of the work.

SULK

Playing Hamlet without knowing the lines, just slouching around
disgusted in the corner of the court. Claudius sends over a copy of
the script to me.

LIBERTY

A sailboat cuts across a blue surface with a rectilinear grid of hemi-spherical depressions, the cusps between capped by white. In the background stands Liberty, mouth agape, dropping her book, torch tilted at a crazy angle.

Marcel Duchamp, giving a talk, standing at a table on a loft floor in New York City. A man of eighty, he is as dapper and as fresh as a man of thirty, dark hair and an unlined face. Then I am introduced to his father, a man who appears to be in his late fifties.

## UNDERGROUND

Sidetracked onto a subway platform by a duplicitous barker on my way to board the roller coaster, I see among the network of rails gleaming in the dark interchange an outmoded steam locomotive relegated to the menial down here, though at closer range its scale collapses through perspective and it is now clearly an oozy, organic being the size of a small dog, still black and locomotive-shaped, foraging and grazing in the soot and detritus common to the underground railway.

## TWO FRIARS

Two friars, monks in brown cloth, rope belts, a tall one and a short one, walking by apartment house glass doors, turn to face them, take out their combs, and stand combing their hair for a full minute, chatting.

AERIAL

A helicopter ride over Provincetown Harbor, a big working bay
with divers excavating a mud-bank shipwreck, freighters, liners,
sailboats kedging off shoals at high tide. Then down a canyon-like,
Market-like main street of nineteenth-century office buildings, and
a left at its end and up another at rooftop level. Out over Race Point
into the bay, where giant tuna leap and fly out of the water in arcs,
with moonlight glinting off their sides, schools of them visible un-
derwater, the campfires alongshore.

A climb up the outside of a major lighthouse, to the level of the light gallery, where thirty cents admits one to the inside of a slowly turning woven basket thirty to forty feet across, a springy floor, and reed windows that can be parted to let light out at night. By day the view from the window is a foreign urban scene, a cross of a bazaar with downtown Naples or LA's Broadway: multistoried buildings of straw and wood, dirty and cluttered. Thinks: must have seen some goings on: local color. Some jerk starts the basket spinning too fast, and it takes us seven hours to slow it down to where we can get off.

BEAUTILITY

A visit to the Aquarium with my father. There are three tanks. The
first contains many small, eight-to-ten-inch black and white fish that
are emitting electric pulses registered on a voltmeter mounted next to
the tank. The second contains a few medium-sized fish that are pro-
ducing a whistling sound that is audible from a small sonar speaker.
The last contains one huge fish, 'a monster of the deep,' which
apparently makes no signals. My father is peeved that I am slow at
discerning the natural law that is exemplified by these displays.

MIDSTREAM

A hike upriver along an old, weathered wooden bridge running lengthwise midstream. It rises and falls, like the Brooklyn Bridge walkway, and barges pass alongside. The water seems quite shallow beneath it, magnifying a white clam on the bottom, but I'm told the channel is dredged a little ways off to the right. This could be the Hudson, with featureless banks. The walkway is kept up to inspect the channel.

Riding on the daily school bus, in my regular seat near the front, we pass a corner of old New Haven being deconstructed, with the remnants of a second-story-level elevated railroad still visible, and George Mattingly moves up to tell me a literary anecdote about a famous Latin American writer coming to town who lodged in that hotel because of some confusion regarding the 'Cou' sign in front. Not only that, but he pulls out a guidebook and finds the relevant passage. Even on the page, I can't quite make out the name... Ruiz?

A PARTY

A party with overhead tracks of acrobats' rings enabling revelers
to take huge flying leaps, swinging from one end of the enormous
salon to the other, high over the heads of other partygoers. Behind a
curtain at one end a man, with a guard stationed next to him, oper-
ates the hoists and travelers that carry the swingers. He anticipates
every hop and leap, so that each is amplified against gravity, much
like hopping around on the moon, but with hands over head, grasp-
ing rings, and no bulky spacesuit.

STRANGENESS

Car window wipes of Managua cityscape: spread out, sky, big struc-
tures, charm of utter strangeness, self-possessed. Then a large and
faceless institution lurking a few blocks off. I enter a second-story
restaurant where some writer friends have already sat down to
lunch. Kit says the city has already ruined a number of poets. I ask
who, and he names some acquaintances, including Bob Grenier,
who he says has had many particular poems ruined by it. There is
some question of where to put the extra chair, and we never make it
to the food.

SHIPBOARD

Gray twilight, shipboard in the freezing Arctic, so dim the gray water is only a tone or two apart from the gray ice hillside sloping sharply up from it and it's hard to see where they meet. Even the image is frozen, without movement or sound. No one else on deck and only a wire rail keeps me from rolling off into oblivion. Turning away with an inward shudder, it's time to reenter the dramatic mayhem taking shape below.

FLIGHT

After years being weighed down to earth, great leaping and soaring trajectories into treetops, propelling off cyclone fencing trampoline surfaces making noises like monkeys' cages.

## THE CHARACTERISTIC CAFÉ

We decide to eat at the Characteristic Café and head uptown a
few blocks, taking a right on 50th. My father drives the car slowly
through a midblock arcade, suffused with a greenish half-light.
Instead of the normal row of varied retail shop windows, this
arcade is the well-known series of small lunch counters and soda
fountains with 1920s demeanor, posters unmistakably of the era
advertising ice cream and other treats. The warren is deserted, as
on a Sunday, though we drive through the interior in tight turns,
finally parking in one to walk out into a weed- and rubble-strewn
lot to look for the café. The only relief on the flat horizon for sev-
eral blocks is a partly dismantled, one-story hub of what looks like
a former large structure, like the food counter at a drive-in movie.
Peering into its windows, you can't even tell if it was a restaurant.
We ask a few people if that was the 'old Characteristic Café,' but
they don't seem to understand the question.

## MUSÉE MÉCANIQUE

A marvelous mechanical box, with a little key on top to wind the
spring which propels the mechanism. The first action is a little game
of acrobatic balls. The field is sectioned off by incomplete parti-
tions with several doorways. A red ball, apparently wooden and
the size of a gumball, shoots out of a rear chamber and, following
recessed guides at points, knocks a second ball further along its
counterclockwise course of curves and ramps until it returns home
to the rear compartment. The first ball remains at its collision
point to serve as the next projectile. After several rounds, a larger
white ball is brought into play and the mechanism elevates a small
cone-shaped section from the field as the white ball enters it, and it
continues to revolve there until a tiny blue ramp turns to the cone
and the white ball is carried off. With more winding of the key,
the ball field is transformed to a new purpose. A roof extends over
it. Two trains can be seen in the dim recesses to the rear, orange
on the left and blue on the right. Their engines lead them out in
a complex array of sharp S-curves and turnings so that the trains
almost appear to be writhing together like snakes. The trains are
simulated by a fabric, stretched from roof to floor, with the cars and
windows and wheels painted in detail. The fabric is pulled through
guides, the same patterns on ceiling and floor, that determine its
course. The windings become less intricate and soon both trains
are hurtling in a counter-clockwise direction and the mechanism
is simulating the sounds of clashing steel and rushing momentum.
Sometimes the trains stick in the old tracks and need a push from
a friendly hand. At another point, the house framing the railroad
scene folds in upon itself, a neat cottage with a peaked roof, and
goes careening around the floor tracks, leaning in at the curves like

a cyclist and teetering near the edges in exaggerated peril. I'm told this antique, which measures no more than a foot or so in any dimension, costs two factors, by which is meant two hundred dollars.

III

# THE SPOONLIGHT INSTITUTE

THE SPOONLIGHT INSTITUTE

> Days, like fingers, unfold their battalions
> *—Paul Éluard*

1.

I'm tired of being so dismantled
decidedly thudless on hidden springs

when the world always has
an explanation for itself

going in and out of the woodwork
Will it hurt the picture

to make the ether hideous?
Longing leads the past

around to the present and
suddenly some subtle entity

vulnerable to too much time
is supposed to shrink your wig

Why monetize the anomie
and still go through shoes at this age

where nothing is too much trouble
Decisions aren't made

less likely by flash bulbs
less fascinating than floor shows

subsiding into hygiene
eliminate guesswork by speaking

in the language of things
as power messaging creates

a hormone cocktail in your prospects
courtesy of Freud

the spectral getting practical
for a fundamentally bad egg

2.


Is this supposed to be a movie?
The only secrets are taken to the grave

where everyone knows anything
to put everything in perspective

gets ironic in no time
Good hinges make such sad metaphors

with prepositions akimbo
and suchness is no stranger

nose in the cosmos
to alibi glamor

that has a way with thugs
like relativity to a railroad

No matter what folded maps
just barely illustrate memory

all the future does is spoil the present
or change your longitude

to the furtive lands
and look into thought colored eyes

The flight of geese through the drowsy mind
is conducive to sleep

as evening to a caveman
underlaps a substitute world

reminiscent of mist
but studded by intention

to illuminate the air
with eponymous bird

3.


Personality is only a persistent error
to mope like a monument

where cooking takes the place of thought
and the geezer keeps coming back for more

We felt our names erased by peculiarity
as if the mask itself were speaking

about perfection of experience
We moved beyond the need for fact

by access to power
how nomad detectors fuel deal fever

and the satisfactory inexpensiveness of nowhere
seemed like a hand on your heart

or an outward sign of intended bleak
the horizon dissolving at dusk

Eternity of desire is
the bright side of oblivion

whichever comes first
since puppy love bebop madness

has no lessons for the eventless
and things bite back when fascination wears off

The early universe was perfectly fluid
but there isn't as much standby

as there used to be
when the public preferred

their screens silent and
age is replaced by possessions

4.


You've picked up a lot of camping
tricks in the margin of error

legally blind to the nondescript
fluttering home through the half light

much less fun
than chain smoking roll your owns

or a soiled dove
taking shade on borrowed time

or come as your pet aversion
with a houndstooth lining

and no big eyes
left of boom

unpeel like animals
but back to the inventory

Don't get me started
on nervous sleep

accelerating interest in comfort
Say goodbye to meticulous

at humanity's loading dock
The imaginary future

replaces the real one
and delays mood episodes

subtracting adverbs from used literature
with epic as the new awesome

walking through lightning
and other people's dreams

5.


Moving among gnomes
outdoes a blind spot for irony

weak on verbs
the familiar false

as a touchstone
Life is short to go to work

and premeditate the next thought
you're not putting

that atom juice on me
with a word to the wires

that diminish appetite for magnitude
in any kite wind

the mystery of someone else
or remembered wallpaper

just the same as it is in Cincinnati
angling for fiasco

A sentimental nature is welcome
to cheap stunts

that makes things matter
if inside know-how

summons the equipment
to hollow victory

expecting anything
of a stranger

too fast to live
too young to happy

6.


Dreamy improvs lubricate
the machinery of fate

the way sarcasm is a little
out of place in the jungle

cornerless as an end in sight
It's time to move the furniture

but I am not the person to see
about that event horizon

or even think of uncertainty
underneath everything

Since aliens ate my brain
numerous sounds of English

make room for occasional tables
and sudden behavior

the world needs pills against
The worst part's almost over now

that fresh pictures take
steps to smooth maps

while we noodle a glut of tuneage
and the star boarder

dreams of electric soup
I am past work

capital being crystallized labor
so it's okay to blank out

the whole kit and caboodle
One monkey don't start the show

7.


This is an idiodicy
devoutly to be wished


even in her chill zone
a failure on my head


Though each optical illusion
is pronounced dead


in the handed down world
Check check check check


When the abyss looks back into you
very special is not very special


and agency sticks out like tripwire
at the limit of expression


only separated by circumstance
no sleep no soap no towel no breakfast


All this fun is killing me
with spiritual bouquets


at the place near the thing
never mind my malady

or mistaken identity
with green around the gills

Extreme ladies help me
develop current reality tree

through settled affairs
and evaporating clouds

of emotional experience
full of words

8.


Do you not agree with that
which I have said to you now


or have the fantods
run out of veins


in the history of infinity
High winds may exist


like a scratchy crystal set
and I know what's a yacht


Anticipation of outcome
guarantees the absence of grace


Brightness has fallen from my interior air
with false starts galore and imitation empathy


for the ethereal hacker
syncing feeling to digital hugeness


angry and owl shaped
in the diaphanous mirror


that undiscovers solitude
in a crowd of countryside

an emotional Chihuahua
mincing perfectly toward

nothing in particular
Old men in old hats

I used to be contemplative
but now just complain

and can't help pointing out
what is hidden beneath things

9.


I'm tired of pretending I'm not
a bitch-ass rock star from Mars

escaping from underneath
the unanswering machine

without philanthropic avenues
and a deep passion for steam

Beauty operators command good money
and tough is putting mildly

the treatment you're going to get
as authors in eternity

Where the Weeds Are
West Eats Meat

The Ultimate Tiara
But is the unironic vocative even possible today

with cities measured in forgiveness
Music is among the better things

transparent little knobs on our temper
while remembered dreams are reuptaken

by the unconsciousness and forgotten
as it was the Indian manner

to vanish into the landscape
with a minimum of indolence

containers of American atmosphere
shipping westward

Everything I feel is like a magnet
This isn't the mother of all anything

10.


Ineffable socialites are in me
playing for creeps I mean keeps

and syncretizing traces of individuality
There is no reason to bring

the electrician in on our troubles
once the museum is gone

nostalgia a sickness of the physical
memory until it isn't

(sorry I'm trying my best)
England without lettuces

Tudor to the max
Kiss it forever goodbye

It's only the tango you love
hoping to make a visible dent

unconvinced that nothing actually exists
kernel panic in the physics package

and no time to spare
regarding second sight

a hare's breath beyond the pale
of negative concord

I've been getting ready to write
this my whole life

several acres of destination
providing a limbo of contingency

in the course of the day
my last password nature's god

11.


I'll take one Ahab hat
for each operating phaeton

having a ball in the object
garden back of beyond

seeing more complicated things
with fewer aesthete inputs

Say a word for the parlor maid
to make a spectacle of self

and unring the wrecking bell
of mind under matter

I could have been a waterfront character
but overactive logic bloweth where it listeth

with breathless personal instants
and three quarters of a million chances

to get the next word wrong
where wonders soon wane

in the stillest landscape
only a model train moves through

Now dark matter's not
made of tiny black holes

Our call sign
harm's way

Be a beauty
to your soldier boy

Prohibit container lift
body touching here

12.


The flea circus feels lonely without me
injecting particularity in dead air

and speaking roughly
defuses party sparks

like disappearing cigarettes
in carnal life

Lower code overhead
Ruby on Rails

is music to social lemurs
but mutant ear cats

have more street smarts
compact of jars

Why use my place as a springboard
for the upper air in translation

becomes words to that effect
Let philosophical zombies

entertain the troops
with mood lighting

Most other suave
belongings outlast flasks

be it for lack of show
scopcraft or wallet litter

While Clio muses
on exaggeration cards

unstrung signals tell
me like you mean it

13.


The world is always classical
in the sequel of events

How come vicious rubes
can't accidentally hear

the zeroes screaming in
Minutes of syrup

Use your mentality
to make a living effervescent

I'm not a country dumpling
and too many sad ducks

begin to feel the shell
to keep regret away

Can shadows limit confusion
by spreading stealth

Wandering scribes consume vocabulary
with handkerchiefs for goodbye

spirited through sewers
letting worry get after one at times

What just happened
called like innocence

on body of work
We are but as grass

despite this dream job
bugging off into space

I'll have the cathode soup
followed by a cheese amulet

*From Nature* was designed by Kyle Schlesinger and typeset in Sabon at Cuneiform Press in the autumn of 2018. There are 500 copies, of which 26 were lettered and signed by the author.